Aloneness

Aloneness

UMELO OJINMAH

Copyright © 2021 by Umelo Ojinmah.

Library of Congress Control Number:		2021910838
ISBN:	Hardcover	978-1-6641-7733-8
	Softcover	978-1-6641-7735-2
	eBook	978-1-6641-7734-5

All rights reserved. No part of this book may be reproduced or transmitted in any form or by any means, electronic or mechanical, including photocopying, recording, or by any information storage and retrieval system, without permission in writing from the copyright owner.

Any people depicted in stock imagery provided by Getty Images are models, and such images are being used for illustrative purposes only.
Certain stock imagery © Getty Images.

Print information available on the last page.

Rev. date: 05/28/2021

To order additional copies of this book, contact:
Xlibris
844-714-8691
www.Xlibris.com
Orders@Xlibris.com
830996

Acknowledgements

This book could not have been possible without the active encouragement of Professor Thelma Obah. She nudged me more times than I can count to write again. When I started, she graciously read and edited the works as they came along. I owe her much gratitude in more ways than one. I also want to thank Helga Jnr Ojinmah for her assistance with some of the editing.

My thanks goes to the following friends and relations without whom this book would probably not be published: Engr Felix Eze, Dr Andy Brockenbrough, Nze James EzeOkeke, Mr Ferguson Adesoye, Pastor Ndukwe Chinaka, Okezie Eze, Dr Ikechukwu Apakama, Nze Obim Ojinmah, Helga Jnr Ojinmah, Nze Okey Chigbu, Nze Jasper & Dr Ihuoma Ofoma, Arnold Umelo Ojinmah, Simi Obe, Dr John Ojinmah, Ben Tyndale Opara, Jessica Wright, and a host of others too numerous to mention in this limited space. Thank you all.

I want to specially appreciate my Wife, Obum Chinyere; my son, Arnold Umelo; and daughter, Praise Ebube, for the joy and peace they bring daily into my life. You are the air I breathe. Love you all so much.

All glory goes to my Lord and Saviour Jesus Christ for keeping His covenant.

Umelo Ojinmah
(Seattle WA)

Contents

I

Dance of the Spirits 1
Ofo na Ogu 3
Fireside 7
Ajani: Earth-Goddess 9
Initiation 11
Boa: Water-Goddess 13
Propitiation 15

II

Atonement 19
Race of Life 21
Wait For Me 23
Agugua (Consoler) 25
Season of Emptiness 27
Blame Game 29

III

The Gardener 33
Anchor 35
Obumneke 37
You Take my Breath Away 39
A Dance With You 41
Apart Blues 43

IV

Mother 47
The Visit 49
Re-Union 51
Love That Hurts (for Dexter) 53

V

War of the Gods 57
Hope Alive 59
I have Seen 61
Laugh at Death 63
Prayer 65
Salvation 67
Jesus I come 69
Today's Spirit 71
The Supplicant 73

VI

Be Still 77
Palms 79
One Drop 81
Iyi Aza (Stream) 83

VII

Stranded 87
Strange Friends 89
Hold on 91
Birthplace 93
Time 95
Why 97
He Married Him 99
Waiting Room 101
Aloneness 103
Not ... alone 105

VIII

EmmAnam (for Poet Emmanuel Anametemfiok) 109
The Dance (for Ken & Totti Ndukwe SAGS Old Boys) 111
Mother Hippo's Call (for Old Boys of SAGS) 113

IX

Bleak Moments (Mourn for Democracy) 117
Political Jobbers 119
Oh My Country 121
Trivial Wars 123
Needless Sacrifice (Lt Agubata 27thDec 1969) 125
Never Again: Biafra 127

X

Remnants 131
They've Come Again 133
AK47 Fodders 135
The man inside 137
Hand of God 139

I

Dance of the Spirits

The eerie flute that summons masquerades from the grove
Dangles in the air, tremors for humans.
The ring-eyed dancer entertains,
While the spirits congregate.
"Oti nkpu"[1] scatters the crowd
in mock display of power until Agaba[2] arrives.
Boys don't tangle with men;
Oti nkpu slithers out of the arena.

The beloved maiden masquerade
May dance to the flute and ogene, metal gong,
But the ikoro[3] is for Agaba dance
Until the arrival of "Ijele"[4].

Majestic king of masquerades,
Esoteric voice prophesying peace.
Our yam barns are full
Our children are joyful
Your steps calm the land
Our world is at peace.

---

[1] Oti nkpu is a notoriously rowdy masquerade. Used for crowd control.

[2] Agaba is a middle level masquerade. Often carved to have two faces.

[3] Ikoro is the biggest wooden slit-drum. It is usually stationary because it is too big to be moved.

[4] Ijele, dubbed the king of masquerades, it is a majestic colorfully decorated big masquerade. Because of its size and weight. It dances slowly ever mindful of where to place its feet lest it falls.

Ofo na Ogu[5]

For ages I watched
the rising sun suffuse
Dada's face as he begins
the morning ablutions without
which nothing is done.
Striding water bowl between knees
right hand dips into water:
Ejim Ofo[6], he proclaims -
that symbol of authority bequeathed,
ordained headship and intermediary
that empowers intercessory obligation.

Each day brings its baggage, he continues
"Eke kere Uwa"[7] creator of the world,
I stand at your gate, a supplicant
For me and family both far and near:
May we not go out
when the roads are famished for blood,
A child carrying nothing breaks nothing.
May the circle of life not be broken in my time:
Eke![8] I greet you. May our barns be full and our wives fruitful.
Orie! I greet you. May our progenitors clear obstacles on our paths.
Afo! I greet you. May we bequeath our descendants, peace,
prosperity and knowledge of good and bad;
and the wisdom to tell the difference.

---

5. Ofo na Ogu encapsulates the concepts of staff of traditional authority, power, justice, equity and uprightness
6. Ejim Ofo a proclamation that he is the custodian of the symbol authority and justice.
7. Eke kere uwa Creator of the earth.
8. Eke, Orie, Afo and Nkwo are the four market days that constitute Igbo calendar. All activities revolve around these four days.

Nkwo! I greet you. May our children follow in the eternal path
that ensures the cyclical well-being of homestead and clan.

Ejim Ogu,[9] he intones.
That vindication of a righteous
supplicant who comes before the
eternal One with clean hands
for equity and justice.

This is a new day and a new beginning
Our household comes under divine coverage.
My eyes will not see my ears without mirrors.
Everyone that steps out today
returns unscathed.
The food we eat will nourish us,
The water we drink will refresh us.

Eke kerem, my creator, I stand in the gap
for those you gave me.
Rub their feet with oil,
Open their eyes to see good
Protect them from evil.

As I wash my hands, cleanse me
of blood guilt of my progenitors.
As I wash my face, brighten my day and life.
As I sprinkle this water on my feet,
it takes me into your path and fatness.
Igwe ka Ala,[10] Heaven is greater than the earth.
We solicit your divine presence and lead.

As Dada breaks the Kola-nut, a complement
of the ablution rites, he tosses a piece out:

---

[9] Ejim Ogu is the spiritual essence that activates the Ofo indicating Equity, truth, uprightness and righteousness.

[10] Igwe ka Ala Heaven (sky) is greater than the earth.

Our ancestors, come and eat your kola
for we cannot eat without remembering you;
our daily lives revolve around you and the unborn.
The world you handed to us is in good hands.
He tosses a piece into his mouth,
chews noisily and offers me and anyone else around some.

Today I straddle the water bowl.
I look up at Chi Okike[11] who knows all things
and invoke the eternal principle
Ejim Ofo na Ogu
As I pray for those now entrusted to me.
May the circle of life not be broken in my time.
Ise!!!

---

[11] Chi Okike The creator/God

Fireside

As we gathered around the blaze
Our thoughts on the yam roasting,
eyes transfixed on the flame;
My body warmed by both the fire
and thoughts of roasted yam with "ugba"[12] and palm oil;
Nana's voice fluttered in the wind.
The stories followed each other,
some old and a few new ones.
Even the old stories sounded new
as more twists and embellishments are added.
I don't know which magnet drew us more,
the stories or the roasted yam.
But the full moon season
was always one of fun for us.
As I steadied my gaze on the flame,
figures seem to dance in my eyes
transforming from one thing to another.
It was enthralling images,
and cocooned in my thoughts time stood still;
only the images moved.
Nana periodically turned the yam,
never allowing any one part to be charred.
It was mechanical from practice.
But that was lost on me as my eyes played games with the flames.
Today, as my mind floats to those times of innocence,
I rue what our children are missing.

---

[12] Ugba is Oilbean seed

Ajani: Earth-Goddess[13]

At the beginning of time
Chi Okike, the creator made you the supreme deity.
He beckoned on you and from you
he formed the first man,
making you supreme above others.

From the beginning of time
we came from you and
each succeeding generation
returns to you for rejuvenation
in the circle of life.
When the umbilical cord is buried
it is a supplication for your benevolence
to your offspring.

When the elders pour libations
you are the first to drink your fill.
Only after you will others queue.
When our eyes close and our job is done,
it is to you that we return.

Embrace us in the land of the living
for Mother Earth is without end.
Every being steps on you
After flying in the air
we plant our feet on you for grounding.
Ferrying across the oceans
our feet return to Mother Earth.

---

[13] Ajani Earth Goddess or Mother Earth is the custodian of mores; social norms.

So, this day, I petition Ajani
Supreme goddess of the earth
for benevolence and protection
against every other force out there
for all your children.

Initiation

As bleeding eve turns dusky
Nimble, sure footed youngsters emerge
At quick pace, animal calls guiding
In blanket pit-darkness they move.

Fear, knots stomachs, poised like darts
Lurking in their hearts…these boys
About to become men.
Enkindled embers sterilize ancestral tools
Incision deepens, blood spurts;
Bleeding remnant shrinks into scrotum.

Satiated, face aglow
Priest cackles for no shriek
Broke the vigil
Broke the spell
New man, of form transits.

Distant growl of thunderclaps
Amadioha, the god of thunder
Gorges on oblations
We clap, thunder claps
Hearts overflow with pride
Weary, boys who left
Return as men of the clan
As dewy dawn turns light.

Boa: Water-Goddess

As dusk turns to night, priest watches as the water maiden
slithers out of its hole on her daily pilgrimage.
Weaving spiral paths, crawling belly on sand.
Oh! mermaid remember your promise priest intones.

In mystery of noon
When morning's battle is lost,
resting, drowsy on offals
Do not take this only kernel.

At twilight, sun is overcome
Fatigued and weary from onslaught of darkness, bows.
As you embark on your nightly pilgrimage
O mermaid remember the supplication of your priest.

II

Pitch darkness heralds dawn
Lone traveller leans on mistaken trunk,
swift curls muffles futile shriek
Sleep laden eyes widen
As mermaid's jaws widen.

Shadow hugs the feet at noon.
Child's absence scalds mother
as she hastens to the priest.
When weaklings turn to leopards
The world, like a boulder perched
On the edge of a precipice tumbles.

Priest's divination bewilders mother.
A dog does not eat the bone hung on its neck, she moans.
This lone kernel, wrung from flaming embers, gone in mid-life ... gone.
Incensed, priest sharpens knife and waits for vengeance
on renegade goddess as she crawls home at dawn.

Propitiation

Ceaseless wailing of the baby
Four market days;
No appeasement from mother's milk.
Dada paced, down and up, eyes red.
He consulted "anyika"[14]
Famed medicine man from across the river.

Anyika poured out his beads on the raffia mat.
Turned them ever which way;
Made incantations and a brew
As wailing grew louder

Desperate dada went to "agwo turu mbe"[15] dreaded medicine man.
He came with pomp, jangling the metal staff
Eyes ringed with white chalk and red clay.
Discomfiting visage did not appease baby
Weak and listless, the child moaned
Exhausted from crying.

Agwo turu mbe's demand:
A female goat, ten tubers of yam, a bag of cowries, was a small price.
Midnight, the hour of communion
Between the living and the dead
In the middle of the four-forked road
Carrying baby, mother inconsolable
trudged behind dada

---

[14] Anyika Famed traditional medicine man reputed to do the near impossible

[15] Agwo turu mbe A snake that strikes at the tortoise only strikes the shell. A moniker for people who claim that nothing an enemy does can harm them.

The propitiation was long:
A few incisions, rubbed with "nzu"[16] and "uhie"[17]
Agwo turu mbe sent incantations
To "Eke kere uwa" sacrificing a white cock
In ransom for a soul gone to the maker
Dada returned at dawn to bury his son.

Agonized dada brought all paraphernalia
Inherited and acquired to accompany child
Holding his wife, they prostrated
before the Pastor for baptism.

---

[16] Nzu Bentonite edible clay

[17] Uhie Yellow or red colored chalk

II

Atonement

My son, you have heard me say
Curse causeless cannot come.
There are immutable laws in heaven and on earth.
The offense that brings the wrath of the gods
may seem trivial to the uninitiated;
but for each transgression there is appropriate propitiation.
Some require a cock, some a goat or even a cow;
others the ultimate sacrifice of human blood for expiation.

When Chi kere uwa, the creator,
watched his creation wander blindly
He summoned the heavenly hosts
to deliberate on remedy.
Everyone realized that these excesses
could only be rectified by blood atonement;
but none was willing.

It grieved Chi Okike, the creator,
that no one would sacrifice
for mankind but they consort with them.
As He grieved, the prince to the throne,
embraced His father and stepped up.

I have assessed my many children;
You are not covetous and you make peace amongst your siblings.
So, I declare: no one born by a woman will be able to hurt you;
every incantation and sacrifice offered the gods
for your head will be rejected.
Today, your ikenga is exalted
above your peers and all adversaries.
I ask only of one thing my son;
keep your hands clean.

Race of Life

At nineteen an elderly uncle beckoned;
Son, you are about to be a man.
Every man runs a different race,
the offsprings of envy are poisonous.

The push and pull of fame and riches have fangs.
The gods ordained for each a lane:
Both the tortoise and antelope
got to Noah's ark in time for the sail.

I looked at his face,
a mischievous smile hovering at the corners of his mouth;
"why are you telling me this?" I asked.
Because, someone who is carrying no pot
does not break one.
Your feet and hands are clean, keep them so.
The constant guardians that draw favor from gods are truth and clean hands;
against them there is no shield.

It's been many years now.
My son is about to be a man;
I have searched but there is no better wisdom
to bequeath him.
There is an ebb and flow to wealth and fame
I have watched the rich beg for food and Generals cry.

People have bent the truth,
thrown it in the dustbin of life,
scorned and weary it has always emerged
to sit in judgment over them.

So today, I tell my son:
embrace and hold truth dear;
keep your hands clean and you will stand
on their shoulders to become whatever
your Chi[18] has ordained.

---

[18] Chi. Personal god

Wait For Me

I shall not be "Nturumokpkpo"[19] the wood-pecker,
whistling away while the mother was alive,
in preparation for her demise and funeral,
only to be thwarted on the day by a boil on its beak.

I shall not be the deer, kin of antelope,
master dancer, bounding, preening
in preparation for a dance,
but crippled on the d-day.

I shall not be the tortoise
Late at every occasion,
Crawling in after guests have left
his own marriage ceremony.

Wait for me, my friend;
The waltz we started has only just begun.
Before the end of the rainbow,
we shall dip our feet again in oil;
Lord over mounds of fufu[20] and bitter-leaf soup,
and wipe our mouths with frothy fresh palm-wine.

---

19   Nturumokpokpo. The wood-pecker bird
20   Fufu Pounded yam traditionally eaten with variety of sauces/soups

Agugua (Consoler)

It brewed in the womb of time
they said it will not be
Knees calloused from constant supplications
had pierced the heart of God
Even when they said it will not be.

I wake every morning oblivious
that the awakening had begun.
Taunts have been my food;
from friends who smirk
and snigger behind my back.

For six years we kept going to the well.
I could not have borne it;
but he carried the greater weight,
fending off everyone for my sake.

Hope runs eternal, they say.
Disappointment turns to sadness
when Hope is not fulfilled.
So, I curled myself into a ball,
my brow hot and pounding.

I must have passed out
His unanswered calls brought panic.
I woke up in the hospital;
he had the widest smile.
Why would he smile when I am sick?

They said it will not be,
but the doctor said something
was brewing in the womb.
So, in the fullness of time
what they said will not be, came to be.
I named him Agugua,[21]
for he wiped away my tears.

---

[21] Agugua Short form for Agugua m'akwa. The one who wipes away tears from the eyes of the burdened.

Season of Emptiness

The beckoning of the Ikoro,
Used to herald the season:
Pulsating deep in the jungle,
Young men file from the enclave.

The gathering of the clan,
Where rippling sinews test age old contest
between two tortoises to know which is male,
has become mockery and ribbing.

Mothers bemoan the clandestine
Rustling of the hatchery,
Reminiscing days secluded
For the "egwu onwa",[22] moonlight dance,
Away from prying eyes of adolescent lust.

Only loafers stray to the secret maiden dance;
Manliness wrapped in raffia palms,
Await the new masquerade hidden in the grove;
Boys now turned men jostle;
Challenging to don the hood of Agaba masquerade.

The whack of cane on bare skin
Shrugged off as men square,
Taunting each other to defend their ikenga.

---

[22] Egwu Onwa translates as moonlight dance but its significance is more than children dancing during a full moon. It is also the period that women secluded themselves to learn new songs and dance steps for the many festivities of the year.

Today, fathers stare with unseeing eyes
At the future of their children without a past;
Young men now pounding fufu
While the heath is cold.
The manly tingling in their bones
Unanswered in this season of emptiness.

Blame Game

They say, where a crying child is pointing,
you will find either the mother or father.
Children bend to training,
but learn from parents' behavior.
What we put in a child
determine the adult we foist on society.

This Nanny's generation
un-parented by eight to fivers
waking up to hustle children to school;
Nanny takes over from school.
Children asleep by the time parents return;
and the cycle continues.
They turn around to decry society
wondering what has gone wrong
with the world made up of people parented by Nannies.

They say, age brings wisdom
that a person may have more
clothes than the parent
but can't have more rags.
... that was yore
these days, some people
wear costly rags, deliberately
torn in all and every place,
to reveal all and everything.
So yes, a person may have
more rags than the parent
for what some people are wearing are rags.

So, when I see a young lady
all but naked, and people gawk
I walk on wondering
whose daughter she is.
To us all, parents:
What you see around you
are seeds we planted
For they say, "curses are like chickens,
they always come home to roost",
and the good book says:
"They sow the wind, and reap the whirlwind." (Hos 8:7)

III

The Gardener

He planted a bed with roses
At bloom time he went to pluck some for his table.
The thorns pricked his hands
His blood was redder than the rose

So, he planted another bed
and improved the stock.
Gone were the thorns
and each bloom season he had roses for his table

His neighbor envied his garden
and planted two gardens
and went about his business
At bloom time he went to pluck
some roses for his table
The weeds and thorns bled his heart
Why is my bed not as good as yours? he asked the Gardener.

I work hard to beautify my garden.
I improved the stocks,
weed and prune them everyday.
Under the sun and rain, I toil.
As in love it returns my gift of time.
You get out of life and love
what you put into them.

Happiness in marriage and love
is nurtured daily by open affection,
truth and commitment until they bloom.
A couple in love is a joy to behold
... I know...

Anchor

Growing up I was told:
when the hand can't find support
it rests on the knee.
Socialized to believe
that everyone needs an anchor,
I watch youths flounder;
oriented in their self-sufficiency,
they believe they don't need guidance:
not from parents or teachers.
They are told that the world is theirs
to explore and exploit.
In a society where parents and mentors
are jailed for mentoring, chaos prevails.

Watching what they have made
of this inheritance,
someone needs to remind them
that a ship without an anchor will drift and flounder.
Our lives require stabilizing anchors
for stars fade as fame; and status diminishes with time.

I have seen many an anchor:
parents in my youth,
always there through thick and thin.
Then a few good friends along the way,
Some stick for a while, others flit away.
With luck a mate that sticks to the end;
but when your mate becomes a friend,
the anchor is blessed and fortified
to weather any storm.

When ocean waves rise,
and turbulence roars,
you need an anchor to hold firm:
not letting you drift
not letting you sink
buoyed by unwavering faith
you bobble to the top.

Obumneke

Our paths crossed near the oil bean tree
Your long neck and longer strides bewitched me.
My eyes roved, following your steps.
I could not turn away.
Like a hooked fish I struggled but to no avail.

Once bitten, I cautioned myself;
I opened my mouth and gulped air
When I talked to you, I could feel
The wings of the angels.
Your voice was the cascading brooks on rocks.
The thrill filled my heart with joy

It seems like yesterday my love
That first kiss that sealed my fate
To love you with all of me
To hold and never let go
That you said 'yes' is still a miracle
But it was ordained by the oracle

Decades have passed my love
Years ebb and flow
But your beauty remains
Ethereal and ageless queen
Mother of our children
I love you today more than ever
...Obum...

You Take my Breath Away

I woke up with the sun in my face.
Bright and early, I seek His face;
Remembering you, for His grace
abounds even in this phase.
You take my breath away.

Yesterday because of His grace
You came into my embrace.
What would I have done in this race,
Without His grace?
For you take my breath away.

Today I look up with the sun in my face,
Knowing that in your sweet embrace,
I see His face.
For you, Obum my darling,
Take my breath away.

A Dance With You

The flutes are silent
as the drums and ogene,
the metal gong whose rings
pierce a dead's ear;
For today we shall dance
to our own music.

The longing in your eyes
and the ring of your laughter
are music enough my love
Standing here with you
gazing at the emerald sky
Beautified with a million stars
Like diamonds on a crest
of dark hue, they glow as you do
For today my love
we shall dance to our own music.

Our morning was graced with dews from the creator.
At midday He poured out honey in abundance
Into our open mouths.
We drank to our heart's content.
Basking in this love so bestowed
with overflowing kindness and grace.

As we transit to late afternoon
I celebrate the products
of this union.
I often ask what would have become of me
if our paths had not crossed
On that fateful day beside the oil bean tree?
The answer is still nebulous.

Apart Blues

I count each second of each minute
These many years apart
Wonder, this hot aching love
Same today as when it began

Each day begins the same
Lifted clean hands beckon
The all-knowing for His blessings.
As I plod through the day
Your thoughts keep me grounded.
As I ease the load off my feet
Before eyes close for rest,
Hands are lifted in thanksgiving

Memories are banks from which we draw love
for each passing second; for daily sustenance.
The zillions of love deposits
We made each passing day
are what keeps fresh:
Your every smile.
The little nothings that watered our lives
I draw from for each day.

Not the big bangs of emotion and passion,
But the gentle touches as we stroll.
Whisperings of Cupid in the ear;
Cuddling under the mango tree;
Sweet nothings carelessly tossed in the wind;
Are banks now paying dividends.

As the anniversary of our "apartness" approaches,
I can't believe it's been this long my love.
Yet each morning I wake
With smiles on my face
Knowing that this-
This love of ours
Sustains me another day.

IV

Mother

Even in the heat of anger,
a doting mother does not hurl hurtful words like bricks when scolding a child.
Words are seeds and each seed produce after its kind.
Children forgive but may not forget those words
that seared their soul, cutting deep like knives.

A mother's love is a soothing balm,
a calmative that has peace and joy as companions.
It is both food and investment:
Children eat and live for it.
It multiplies and yields dividends.
It is in the breast milk that nourishes,
in the cozy crook of the arm that cradles the child.

It is in the peculiar scent that makes a child
distinguish mother from others,
and the absolute trust and leap of faith
which a child bestows only on a parent.
For a mother is a special animal.

The Visit

The twinkling in her eyes were a thousand stars.
She was truly a sight for sore eyes;
It's been a very long while since I beheld
those dimpled cheeks always ready to break into a smile.

As I looked into her eyes, I saw the sadness
lurking behind the smile.
We had never been separated
for more than a few months before;
and here we are after a period of three years.

What a mark three years can leave
on growing tendrils.
The baby eyes had been replaced
by the mature gaze of a young woman
ready to take on the world.

The magnitude of the lost three years
of her life became apparent when she held my hand
as we were wont to do and said:
I have missed you so much dad.

It was no more a baby hand;
it was no more holding for reassurance;
it was the firm hand of assurance.

Re-Union

Nature abhors vacuum, they say;
and nothing stands alone, our elders concur.
I may not be ancient but Iroko[23] is a loner.
In its aloneness it towers above other trees.
Habitat of eagles, whose plumes
adorn the caps of the honored.
But man was not made to be alone.
Loneliness is kinsman of misery;
Chi Okike ordained that man should not be alone.
The woman was created to wife the man;
be companion and remove loneliness.
The children are insurance
of replication for mankind.
Nothing compares to the joy of parenthood;
the harmony of disparate voices,
and togetherness of individuals.
Only nature's anvil could forge concinnity
from the chaos of children with disparate temperaments.
This unique peace cocoons family.

Separation brings its own agony;
not only of lonesomeness even among people,
but undefinable longing and deep heartache.
Such is nature that only re-union
can assuage this ache.

Seeing his face after so many years,
my heart was pounding in my ribs
like the joy of first love.

---

[23] Iroko African Teak tree

His broad smile drank the whole world
yet was fixed on me alone.
The magnet that drew us into each other's arms
was stronger because of the separation of time.

The filial love that flowed was tangible.
A thousand stars danced in our eyes
as we looked at each other;
and drank the air as elixir.
We knew the re-union will be short;
but time is of no essence with love.
This special love of a son reunited with his father.

Love That Hurts (for Dexter)

I am two generations removed,
From the light toned skin of the beautiful boy
that came into my life.
With a face only reserved for angels,
he had issues from day one;
but dearly loved notwithstanding.
Would have gone to the ends of the world
and back to see that rare smile;
often wry I thought,
but who can decipher the thoughts of an angel.

He came like the wind;
two seasons and some he tarried,
and vanished like the spirit he was
leaving a gaping hole where my heart used to be.
He was beyond handsome;
beautiful, many said, for a boy;
with a smile that he flashes occasionally,
and bestows like benevolence.

So many years have gone by
yet I still wake up in the night
longing to hold him one more time;
to see that fleeting wry smile one more time.

V

War of the Gods

When Chi Okike created the gods
He also created man.
Each god he assigned specific duties.
One was to protect man, another to provide his needs,
and others for other purposes.

Man, recognizing the importance of the gods
to his well-being began to worship them.
But the gods were always jealous of each other.

So, a man may petition and sacrifice to the god of good health in the morning
to be struck down by the goddess of earth at noon.
In confusion man petitioned Chi Okike.

The gods were summoned
At the assembly, commotion ensued
For the god of death claimed that he was stronger
than Chi Okike and would not take his orders.
"Even though Chi Okike creates, but I take his creations at will," he boasted.

The gods were split. Some sided with the god of death
in anger Chi Okike banished them to the underworld.
Out of spite, the goddess of earth bargained with the god of death
to receive every one he takes and sided with him.

Chi Okike, in obedience to the law he himself enacted could not kill a god.
So, he consulted with his first born, heir to his throne.

Who girded himself and armed with his flaming sword
defied the goddess of earth and passed through her domain
to confront the god of death.
The battle was fierce; seven days and seven nights they fought.

On the seventh night, the son of Chi Okike
pinned the god of death to the ground,
raised his flaming sword to slay him when he remembered the law.
So, he bound him and plucked the keys of eternity from him.
So, the righteous will not remain dead forever.

Hope Alive

His words told me to look unto the hills,
But among valleys and rivulets I wallowed.
Caught in the jungle of life
I sought solace in caves, dwelling in solitude.
The many faces I saw a blur
Wondering when ... I slept

Dawn's rays caressed my face,
A yawn and I am awake
Beholding the golden radiance
Of the hill awash with the sun
I looked up and it was a new day.

My spirit soared as I beheld the beauty
Of the rising sun and hope.
I knelt in pure adoration
Of the beauty beheld

The songs of the birds, mournful yesterday;
glorious and heart-warming have become.
One with the universe
I looked unto the hills
And saw my salvation.

I have Seen

There's a depth beyond depth
The dwelling of God's eternal love
From which it flows to the initiates
who have dipped their tongues
in the nectar.

I have plumbed the heart of God
Indwelling of the eternal essence
Love so incomprehensible
The heart is one with Him
For therein love dwells.

Yes, I have seen the face of God
For I have seen love ... true ... pure.

Laugh at Death

I have drunk the cup of affliction
I have plumbed the depth of despair
I looked at the face of death and laughed

In the darkness that is beyond dark
I saw a flicker of light
As I walked it became a blazing fire
blasting its radiance on my face

Basking in its warmth
I stretched forth my hand
And the fourth man in the fire said:
You have been standing in the miry clay too long,
step on this solid rock; I did.

Prayer

As the sun banishes morning dews
So, laughter, sadness.
I will eat joy and laughter
To nourish my marrows.

Humility guarantees longevity, the toad cautions;
jumping helter-skelter cripples the antelope.
As laughter and merriment are foods for the soul,
so stony hearts languish in bitterness.

The breaking of the sun heralds new day.
Master farmer does much work before sunup;
the dawdler yawns at midday.
One who owns the food has bulging cheeks;
but air will be the food for dawdlers.

As gratitude draws favour;
So ingrates scorn, for a bounder is friend to none.
As the early morning sun washes your face
Hasten to harvest good tidings at sunset.

May the oil poured on your head remain fresh.
As you follow the star, let it lead you to the promise.
An elder reclining on a chair sees farther than a child on a tree.
May your strength never wane.

Salvation

At the altar of supplication
one drops burdens of animosity
justified or not.
Salvation is its own cleansing balm;
first step in the new journey.
Offerings dropped before the altar
exchange for blessings dispensed
to hearts that are pure.

A child pursued sighs with relief
at sight of parents,
safe from torment he turns to face tormentors
braggadocios in new found strength
bolstered by trust and belief.

As streams follow established routes
so blessings and curses;
Oblations from patriarchs are generational
umbrellas for progeny.
The coverage from forces known
and unknown which fathers are,
becomes evident when they transit.

Cockroaches emerge from cracks,
tongues that had been silent begin to wag.
Cleansing from ancestral malfeasance is a joy
of salvation and curse breaking,
and a new beginning.

As whetstone sharpens blunt knives,
renewing its life and function;
Salvation reignites man's dead spirit
and energizes the mortal body.
Restoring the joy of father
fighting the descendants' battles.

Jesus I come

Just as I am, I come
Eternal One before you I prostate,
Sobbing and distraught
Unto you I cling Oh Lord
Save me from my sins.

Change my life my God
Have mercy on your creation
Remember your promises.
Infallible One remember,
Show mercy, save your inheritance
That my mouth will laugh again.

Spirit of the living God
Avenge me of my adversaries who
Vex my spirit and embitter my soul.
Enlarge my portion, fulfill your promise
So that my cup will run over.

In total surrender to you Oh Lord,
Not disputing your overlordship;
Down on my knees I bow
Eternal One in total submission,
Every fibre in me yielding
Dear God, to your majesty.

Today's Spirit

As the sun rises each morning
Ushering a brand new day;
Minted in the dark of the night
with blessings for each day
Our spirits open in benediction.

Our hearts yearn for mercy and grace for each day;
New each morning they descend
from the throne of grace to assuage the hunger in our souls.

Though we live one day at a time;
His embrace renews our strength
Suffusing our spirit with peace and knowledge
that in the midst of the storm, we are safe.

The tremors and fears of yesterday are gone;
this is a brand new day.
We live today and our spirit rejoice:
Renewed, refreshed and rejuvenated
we take one step after another
knowing that our final destination is ordained.

The Supplicant

Our ancestors prescribed for every infraction,
a commensurate appeasement.
A fresh pot of soup seasoned with a cock,
for a woman who offends her husband;
A white goat for infractions against Ani, the earth goddess;
A she-goat for someone desiring fruits of the womb;
A goat and accessories for serious infractions against the clan;
and a cow for weighty wrongs against the bloodline and the earth.
But they reserved the ultimate sacrifice of atonement with human blood,
for such sacrileges that are almost unforgivable.

So when we transgress,
the appropriate sanctions
are imposed by the community
for harmony and the ease of our spirit.

But when you called me
you said you have atoned for me;
that I should dispense of my old beliefs.
So I come as a supplicant before you,
requesting total redemption:
and delineation from ancestral lineage.
You don't require a cock or goat;
neither cow or money,
but that my heart be true
and my desire pure.
I've come Lord as a supplicant;
infirm and weak.
Make me whole again
according to your promise.

VI

Be Still

In the gentle gurgling of the stream
you can find the quietness
that calms the soul.
Looking at sunset,
creation resplendent in its richness,
the spirit lifts, becomes one with the universe.

The small enchanting voice
that whispers into the ears
is heard in the stillness of mind and spirit.
The in-dwelling spirit clams up
in a boisterous environment;
so, I go to our meeting place,
the spirit and I, to that place
where he tells me of today and tomorrow.
In meditation he tickles me with tantalizing hope;
rekindles joy bringing sunshine.
When my mind is agitated,
I curl in the cocoon as my spirit communes
with the eternal One for illumination.

Palms

Soothed by the gentle breeze
I watched the dance
Slim and tall the two palms stood side by side.
Their height dwarfed other surrounding palms and trees.
As the breeze picked up they swayed
Mostly in the same direction.
Their trunks never quite touched
but the leaves caressed each other.
It was pleasant to watch as the wind,
now stronger, bent the two palms
in an erotic dance that humored nature.
The knives of countless palm harvesters
have left incisions all over both trunks;
either some careless climber
had carved too deep a foothold on one of the palms
or a woodpecker, looking for nesting, deepened one.
Whatever it was, the wind, now boisterous was too much for one palm
which snapped midway in the dance and the crown fell,
leaving a long trunk shorn of its plumage.
The beauty was gone as the broken trunk stood sentinel to what was not.
Lone palm forlorn still waved in the wind.
I covered myself from the chill
which I had paid scant attention to in my admiration.
Now with the beauty gone,
nature and the landscape lost their allure.

One Drop

I watched as the ink dropped
Spreading its tentacles as it probed
The entrails of blotter
Like octopus, grasping, spreading, engulfing.

The blackness at the center
Lightening as it spreads.
Jagged at the edges, as the blotter
Milked it dry.
So long for a drop of ink

Iyi Aza (Stream)

Its crystal-clear waters
from which we draw for our daily needs,
flow sluggishly, looking deceitfully shallow.
The life of the village interweaves with Aza,
the only source of potable water
in it we wash both our body and clothes,
watching the foamy dirt dance away in bubbles

it's been years but I can still see it now;
carousing all day long in the stream;
fishing for tilapia the size of fingers
yet yelling for joy each time one is caught.

Those were years of our youth.
When the child belonged to the clan
and everyone was his brother's keeper.
Our mother was the village for we ate from every woman's pot.
Often the soup pot was brought out
and we dipped our hands into it with great gusto.
Knowing that a new soup was in the making.
We sang together and often enough slept together
unmindful of whose house we were in when it got dark.

In the morning we would troop to Iyi Aza,
the little brook in the village to bathe but mainly to frolic.
Dipping our mouths to drink from the stream while bathing.
Those were days when the child belonged to the clan.

VII

Stranded

An egret in mid step
one leg hanging in the air
here I stand, stranded
in the midstream of life,
unsure of tomorrow.

I hurl questions in frustration;
curses at the air in impotent anger,
sapped of energy my leaden feet shuffling.
Panic stricken, like a tortoise
I withdrew into my shell.
Then the voice of the spirit came
from the bone of my bone
and to America I went.
Obedience saves life; it saved mine.

As the ancients said,
a man running for his life
sends out distress calls as he runs;
lest the legs fail to take him to safety,
his calls may attract rescue.
The story turned into a scramble
For life saving procedures.
As the planned three months
Stretched to six and beyond;
Objective changed for life.

Sustained by faith and belief
In the supremacy of God and His word
for mankind I know I am part of the master plan.
Holding on to what He told me,
Unshakable in faith, I stand sure
Of my testimony.

Strange Friends

In the journey of life
Our paths cross with many.
One's kith and kin are ordained,
Friends are choice self-gifts.

Some wayfarers are seasonal.
Fading to be forgotten;
Others tag along for a good ride
Until the boat hits an iceberg.
Some will help right the boat for a while.

But in the heat of battles
Floods and the unforeseen
Few stay to see the end
Waving from the shore like strangers.

As air fouled by a wine tapper
Confounds the fly, so conceit of heart, friends.
Beyond flashing teeth,
The blowing wind winnows chaff
And true friends emerge.

Hold on

Jones' springy steps were known
With ebullient sweep,
He steps into a gathering.
A straight shooter some say
Lover of truth others echo

There was a division among his peers;
Not on substance or quality.
Mentoring was his calling;
most welcomed the helping hand
extended to straighten the ladder
on their route to success.

But the green-eyed monster
Lodged and coiled in some,
Would not allow olive branch
extended for system growth.
So Mark thought traps can be set;
unruly behavior has consequence.
He forgot the system is
an elephant, that never forgets.

A mentor once said, documentation
Is the engine of the system;
When you are up, it sustains
your buoyancy or deflates it.
Don't pick quarrels, pick your pen.

So the first reprimand was mild;
almost conciliatory in import,
cautioning about serving the system

as duty and in collective interest.
Mark laughed in his face.

Non confrontation to serial offenders
is evidence of cowardice.
All you do is write your stupid memos,
Mark taunted on Tuesday
So Jones' next memo reminded the system
of the penalty for serial offenders

And the elephantine system
began retrieving and sequencing;
Noting that the limit of three advices,
two warnings, has been tripled;
read the riot act for the statute of limitations
for conciliatory talks had lapsed.

Jones continues to mentor,
to strengthen the system for all.
But the dissident is pounding the
pavement in other places.
Don't let the springs in your steps
Be muted when challenges come.
Hold on and make the system work.

Birthplace

They say where a man is born
does not determine destiny.
They say that even being born
with silver spoons does not ensure success.
They claim that one's parentage
is not a guarantee of pedigree

But a child is the son of a man
Some walk into a room
and they say "oyiri nnaya"
that he resembles his father.
Others come into a room
and people wonder whose child he is.

Good breeding is not in DNA,
But teaching and socialization.
I have watched some parents
give their son everything,
and others nothing but morals.
I have watched the greed
of the new generation;
And wondered what we have done.

A snake's offspring must be long, our elders say.
A lion does not beget a deer
my father told me.
Fish that hops on land
is looking for death
So it is when air is cut
from a man who plunges into the ocean.

Where something is born
determines destiny
A gazelle that jumps into an ocean
is challenging destiny
And a fish that decides to jump
on land begs death
Some people are what they are
because of where they were born.

Language and culture are learned,
And they influence behavior.
Quibbling about this does not change
facts of disposition anchored on birth.

Time

I breeze through the day
unmindful of its existence
and forget time is irrecoverable.
I blissfully waltz through the night
without a care in the world.

Moving with springy steps
bounding over hills and valleys.
The nightingale's voice mingles with mine
in a song to my love.
I inhale the fragrance and aroma
from myriad flowers thankful for life.

My unshorn feet grounded
receives life force linking me with the universe.
The dark blue sky, merges
with the glitter of turquoise spray
of the ocean waves as I stroll
through the shores in this blithely summer.

Free of encumbrances and determined
to relish and savor my youth
I have whirled through life blissfully.

I woke up today and saw
strands of grey as I finger combed my hair.
In consternation I looked at the mirror,
an aged man stared back.
Where has time gone, I wondered
as I sat down on the bed to reflect
on what I have done with my life.

Why

I was not offended by the words
Hurtful as they were,
but the thoughts behind the words.

Nigga is just a word,
the thought that one is inferior informs it.
So, I look for the "why" in what people say.
When heart and mouth are in opposition,
sieve the words for thoughts precede actions.

The words of mindless people have no import
precisely because they are thoughtless.
And thoughtless words mean no harm
because they are air blown to fill space.

What gives words impetus are
the thoughts behind them.
They precede everything.
I am mindful of what people say
because they have minds,
and the mind is devious.

Words, they say, can precipitate war,
what if desire for war informed the words.
Fights are preceded by finger-poking,
which is preceded by the thought of a fight
which itself sprout from the mind.
So, when people talk or act,
I look for the "why" before I respond.

He Married Him

How times change.
Yesterday he married her
to the applause of all.
He brought food from anything he did;
and she cooked food from anything he brought.
When she brings food because he can't,
they claim she married him but society understood
because tides change.

Yesterday the village said and the priest agreed:
man marries woman and chastised those
who reverse the order, for peace in the land.

And day broke and they went to the city.
Something must have happened
for he brought him home,
and the village said NO,
and thrust they out the door.
They went to the priest
who placed a hand over theirs
and he married him.

Waiting Room

Here I sit
In my small world
Watching each person
In their little corners
In their small worlds
Each preoccupied with their issues,
unmindful of the world around.

I turn each time
a name is called,
or a nurse comes,
waiting for my turn
knowing that everyone
will have a turn
to be called.

I marvel at the order;
no raised voices
even in their agonies,
people stoically hold
their tongues and voices
until the unbearable escapes:
and gasps, and painful moans,
wash over the space
as undercurrent of the waiting room.

Aloneness

Betwixt the two polar streams of our existence, at birth and in death, each person is alone.
Each one fills their void with peculiar issues.

That filling, is living.
Its components are family and friends, jobs and works people do.
Each person's route is unique
Even when they seem similar.

Filling with meaningless social interactions, is a gaping hole
of aloneness in the midst of noise and bustle.

Panoramic views lose their allure
when the senses scorn their presence.
Coming home from a boisterous party with friends;
realizing that nothing tangible registered for all the time spent, I knew that I was alone in the midst of people.
Teetotalers don't get drunk, so I can't be accused.
Maybe my mind refused to follow the body to the party, or switched off, but whatever it was, now I know better.

Each day lived is defined by what it's filled with.
They say, you come into the world alone and depart the same.
The laughter and smile that your life brings to another is living.
That laughter, smile and joy become memories long after you are no more.

Not ... alone

Because there are shades of darkness, light is never completely absent in darkness.
The shade of dark is a function of the amount of light within it.
Wherever a person stands, the shadow stands beside.
The acknowledgement of the shadow is a function of the light reflected.
Not seeing the shadow at night is not because of the absence of light but a reflection of the amount of light.
Even when you think you are, you are not alone;
For wherever somebody stands, something stands beside;
Sometimes it's the shadow and others the personal god "chi" assigned to guide and protect.

VIII

EmmAnam (for Poet Emmanuel Anametemfiok)

My friend woke me up with the sounds
of flutes and the talking drum.
The caressing flute cleared the cobwebs of sleep.
I yawned as I reached out for my ogene,
that metal gong that summons the masquerade.
I join you, my friend, in the dance of new birth.

But I must pause for the arena is yours
Our elders say that an old woman
is never too old for a dance of her youth.
The early morning palmwine is frothy
and sweet but its fangs are portent.
As I pirouette I caution myself for the masquerade
should not be unmasked in daylight by missteps.

The Dance (for Ken & Totti Ndukwe SAGS Old Boys)

I said that I will not be "Oturukpokpo" the Woodpecker
who boasted how he will sing down the heavens
At his mother's funeral
But on that day he had a boil on his beak.

Yes, I will not be the antelope
Who made similar boast
about how he will dance at his father's funeral
But on the day of the funeral he was lame.

When Ken dragged one of my feet into the square,
the second followed lamely.
Then Totti massaged, not only the leg,
but my arms and I began to dance.
I said that I will not exhaust my strength
Because the dance has just begun,
but today the dance was vigorous
...exhilarating.

How do you say thanks to the gods?
You go through their messengers.
The sacrifice placed at the fork
Of the road is for the gods
The accompanying invocations
Are mortals' cry for help.
How do you thank the gods when they answer?
Today, not tomorrow, we will
Dance at the village square.

Mother Hippo's Call (for Old Boys of SAGS)

I have dipped my toes
in the dance at the village square,
but the masquerades are dancing
to a different beat of drums.
When my drummer synchronizes
my two feet will dance in the village square.

The dance is for all,
but few dare for it requires a penny;
many have it and are unwilling to give
Others shy away for lack of it.
The call to dance is for all.

Mother Hippo's call is for all
A few have answered the call
Though thousands watch from afar.
Many that would have stemmed her tears,
Stay silent while a few dance.

Today, a friend dragged one of my legs
into the square as the second leg trails lamely;
but this is not a one-legged dance.
We all must dance at the village square
Hippo cannot mother thousands
and moan like an orphan.

I have watched the ants
Master builders and architects,
build masterpieces from bottom up
I have seen ants carry loads many times their size
I have seen them overcome animals

a thousand times their size
I have watched soldier ants
in their organized discipline
Marching towards a common goal
The load may be daunting
but it cannot overwhelm the ant.
I concur: "Ibu anagh anyi danda".

IX

Bleak Moments
(Mourn for Democracy)

Lying at faith's altar I prostrate
When mortals toy with fate
Jingling rosaries that jar ear lobes
Mouthing warped promises
Without ideology or direction

Standing on the stage they splash
Spittles on friends as on foes.
From dawn to dusk transversing
The whole realm blathering
Fake promises and ideologies

Breakers surge, and like reeds
On waves, tossed, we embark
On a futile ride without direction
Led by morons with bags of money
Oh! These bleak moments.

In nakedness of birth I stand
For at baptism, this messiah belch
Alcohol and rancid breath
A nation blighted at birth
Doomed by the curse of Sisyphus

Political Jobbers

Cascading brocade agbada attires
Obscure stomachs contesting
With pregnant women.
Gnarled hands ringed with diamonds poised
Nail coffins of promises;
mouth agape, drooling on putrefied dish
they smack their lips

Incandescent truth exposes the hollow
Promises as they stand on our heads
To reach positions in government.
Kicking aside the ladders they used
To mount Olympia and become
Like Zeus untouchables.

They sit in judgement over us
Even as they prostitute their offices.
Do not ruminate for I told you:
Appropriated finds?
Elevated mediocrity?
Blatant nepotism?
Don't reminisce for I told you.

In the dark void of your imagination
Sprout silvery machinations which
Doomed and blighted even as they bud
Have for product: a failed nation.

Oh My Country

Despots turned Democrats bash
Trust as shackled love slides
From its firm fix
Wrenched from hope on promises
Renegaded even at onset.

Rosy cheeked mediators pocket
The future as potbellied advisers
Traverse Europe and America
Weaving unworkable theories
Laying waste the present and future

Oh my motherland
No balm to salve
The grip of iron teeth devouring
The land
The people
I weep.

Trivial Wars

In ambivalence of lust and innocence
They trudge, fused and primed
Fidgeting for targets;
new slates ready to be violated
By unscrupulous leaders who claim:
We are saints
We are for you
We are the saviours.

Years of deprivations and fighting
With sunken cheeks, wizened faces
They remember pounded foo foo
Of yesteryears, before the killings

Innocent children used as fodders
To satiate the activated lust for power
Of leaders jangling unknown creeds
They tether us, saplings that should
hold up the rafters; now wasted.
Laughter cringes in the land
Made desolate by these trivial wars.

Needless Sacrifice
(Lt Agubata 27thDec 1969)

Sirius gaze not on the scavenging
Of gods who, like Ogun, demand
Mongrels for breakfast.

Priests in dementia invoke
Globules and flakes of human cranium
Exposed by shrapnels gore
On Agubata' side in a futile war.

He in millennium will dole
Waters of Aganippe for he
Will stand guard, watchman at the gate.
He, crucified at noon to satisfy
Fatuous greed, sacrificed.

Mere saplings crucified at Golgotha
Raining brimstone and scalding tears
From mothers in grief;
As they watch the same people
Who gave reasons for war
Sup at table, clinking glasses.
*Lt Agubata died at Umuahia sector of shrapnel
wounds on 27th Dec 1969. He was a friend.

Never Again: Biafra

I watch in amazement the fervor
Of child-men who think war
is pounded yam and vegetable soup,
to bestride and sweat over.

They scoffed at tales they heard:
As old wives tale of the land
littered with the dead,
because the living didn't have
the strength to bury them.
Of people so emaciated that
they were walking skeletons;
Of people crawling because
they didn't have the strength to walk.

As they sit over mounds of pepper soup
with assorted meats they snigger
at the thought of people scrambling
for lizards and rats for meat.
Some snort and declare
how they would destroy any that
challenge their dream of a new homeland.

I watch and I shiver at youths;
fodders for an impending pogrom
already designed, waiting for a trigger.
Oblivious of the gathering storm,
they bark at the moon.

Our elders caution not to come
to gun fights with knives.

Emasculated by government decisions;
stripped of any means of defense,
would they bare their chests
for marauders' bullets?

They chant songs of bravado;
beat their chests in acknowledgement
of their manliness,
but bullets pierce walls I tell them.

X

Remnants

Decades have come and gone
like the ebbs of the ocean on the beach;
leaving debris imprinted on memory.
An inhuman siege on the psyche of a nation.
Physically blocked from the outside world;
daily brutalized by war of attrition,
they sought to grind their souls to extinction.

Forever embedded in our memory
is the stench of starvation,
and the shriveled buttocks of our dying children:
a damnation to an insensitive world
that watched this inhumanity.

The collective sunken eyes
of thousands of dying children,
supplicate heaven for vengeful retribution
to a beastly nation of jackals.
Decades have come and gone
like the ebbing of the sea
washing up on the shores of our conscience
the cruel intention of annihilation.
Like a bad penny, it has turned up
for an encore on the remnants.

They've Come Again

It's not for naught that elders caution mouth:
don't go to war before leg, you risk not returning.
Unbridled tongue, they say, can cause wars.
The boy who shouts: what will he do, what will he do?
is yet to witness a real fight
The clan is preserved when youthful exuberance gives way to sombre elderly advice.
We were warned that fight would not start without fingers poked into eyes.
A hated people walk with caution; but the young ask for how long?
When failed Castrations stare in the face youths strut to claim their heritage.
They say when a woman is treated the same as co-wife, the husband sleeps in peace.
Are these incessant burnings, ploy to begin again?
He who pursues a fowl, is courting a fall.
The leopard is not known to turn from any animal.
When someone is pursued by something bigger, he takes to his heels.
And elders say that he does not stop running till whatever is pursuing him stops.

AK47 Fodders

They know it.
All of them know
their scions are out of reach
Of the unleashed blizzard.
There was no debate
In the house of debates;
when the lord of the manor
made his demands of them.

Some demurred under their breath;
Loud enough not to be heard,
Else marked as saboteurs.
None of their adult children
are within to be harmed they knew;
others shrugged and chewed on their kola nuts.

The caucus meeting was sober
as dossier of everyone's skeletons was unveiled.
The shakers and movers were shaken;
sword of damocles revealed.
None refused to sign the pledge of perdition.

They sold their souls and inheritance;
Enslaving their progeny for posterity.
In nature few animals abandon their young;
so it was with man till late.
Prior generations preserved a future
for their offspring till now.
These politicians eat their descendants.

They watched helpless as hordes of marauders
laid waste their people and lands;
having sold their souls.
The ferocity and barbarism belie
the humanity of the perpetrators.

No whimper came from those
voted to protect their interests.
Castrated and disarmed by their own leaders
they were fodders for the AK47 wielding beasts.
Every dissent was snuffed;
As ghouls ripped the land apart.

The man inside

My response was silence
When the slaughter began.
It is a distant land, I thought.
Then they came to next the town and I was silent.
I was gripped with unease when
a neighboring village was ransacked;
and went to buy bows and arrows.
The man who makes them is no more, I was told.
So I went to buy spears;
Sorry, the town we source them from is in turmoil, they said.
Okay, where can I buy a gun, I asked.
Government has banned guns, they told me..

I bowed my head in tears
as I remembered a story my father told me:
This farmer on his way to farm
saw a tribe of goats in a farm.
It doesn't concern me he told himself
and continued on his merry way.
A few weeks later the goats
had destroyed the farms near the road.
The tribe went deeper, and deeper.
He got to his farm one day
and it had been invaded by the goats.
The time to do something
is when the problem is small, my father said.

So it was that one evening,
they came in their bikes, buzzing like bees.
I woke with the buzz in my ears
and realized that I had been dreaming.

Then I heard that the dream was real; they were coming.
Backed by government they are ransacking villages and towns.
So for the first time in overs sixty years, the Ikoro sounded.

The man inside dies
When its response to abuse;
and endless provocations
Is silence.
And the man inside dies
when a man is physically castrated
by circumstances or powers beyond him.
But the man inside also dies
When he watches his family abused,
and his land desecrated.
So today, in this place, I plant my feet.

Hand of God

For ages they schemed and planned
how to overrun a people, a nation.
They had stripped her naked
and desolate they raped her resources.
But that was not enough;
Humiliated and made prostrate
By decades of starvation of basic infrastructure,
they decided to take her by force of arms.

So, they schemed and planned:
Banned ownership of guns for them
and began importing arms from Turkey
Instead of beautiful fabrics

Youths exchanged shepherd's crooks for AK47s
Strutting both byways and highways
They slung the new cow herding weapon.

Bent on completing an assignment
Ordered by their forbears
to dip the Koran into the Atlantic,
they took their cows to towns and villages.

What grass do cows eat in cities?
People asked and were killed,
Our farms are destroyed farmers wailed
They took both the farms and villages
Killing anything insight.

Now ready and primed
They besieged the cities and waited
for the order to finish what their ancestors started.

The hand of God descended.
The owner of the earth hissed
And a little virus went to work.
The grim reaper began reaping from their leaders
Striking the shepherd and scattering the flock.